Cheerful Chats for Catholic Children

Mrs. Leane G. VanderPutten

DEDICATION

This book is dedicated to my children and my grandchildren who continually enrich my life.

CONTENTS

Leane G. VanderPutten

ACKNOWLEDGMENTS

I would like to thank my family who instils in me the deep desire to be a better Catholic wife and mother.

1. PIERRE AND THE DUCK

One day Pierre's little duck waddled over to Pierre as he was busy mowing the grass on his big farm.

The duck fluffed his feathers to get Pierre's attention. Pierre did not notice at first, but when he saw the duck out of the corner of his eye oddly prancing about, he stopped the mower. The duck looked worried.

Pierre asked the duck, "What is wrong Little Quacking One?"

The little duck quacked and exclaimed, "I am worried that if you cut all the grass there will be none for me to eat! Then all the bugs may fly away because of the noise of your mower."

Pierre grinned, "Silly duck. Look at all this grass! And it will begin to grow again right after I cut it! And the bugs do not go away. They will be right back after I am done with the mowing! You have nothing to worry about, Little Friend!"

Whew! That sure relieved the duck's mind and he waddled back to the pond to take his noon day bath!

We are like that little duck. We worry about many things each day. We don't think things will turn out all right. but we have a Heavenly Father and Mother that takes care of us and we shouldn't be afraid.

Remember what Our Lady of Guadalupe said to Blessed Juan Diego, "***Do not be troubled or weighed down with grief. Do not fear any sickness, anxiety or*** *pain. Am I not here who am your Mother? Are you not under my shadow and protection? Am I not the fountain of life? Are you not in the folds of my mantle? In the crossing of my arms? Is there anything else you need?"*

That means that you can take ALL of your needs to your Mother and she will take care of you.

Always ask your Mother to help you when you are worried. She will turn it over to her Son and They will take care of you!

Let's chat about this: What was the duck worrying about? Why did Pierre grin? Of course ducks cannot talk, but what does this story teach us? Will God take care of us? Who should we turn to when we are worried? Who will she ask to help us?

Prayer: Dear Blessed Mother, we know you are our Mother because you love us so. You even came to earth and appeared to Juan Diego to tell us not to worry. Please help us to remember to pray to you whenever we are worried. Thank you for being our Mother and helping us! Amen.

The duck was happy again,
He didn't have to worry!
He got ready for his walk
Without fear, without hurry!

2. SAMMY AND THE MEDAL

Sammy wandered outside on a lovely fall day. He was looking at the pretty butterfly that was landing on his mother's summer flowers when his eye caught something shiny on the ground. He picked it up and saw that it was his sister Polly's shiny, new miraculous medal she had received for her birthday. Sammy looked around to see if anyone was watching and began to slip it into his pocket.

He then heard his mother's voice, "Sammy! what have you got and why do you look so guilty?"

Sammy sheepishly looked at his mom and opened his hand. Inside his palm lay the shiny new medal that he was about to take.

Sammy's mom reminded him that it was not his to have and that to take anything that did not belong to him was a sin. It was stealing.

Sammy was glad that his mom had stopped him before he put the medal in his pocket. He wanted to be a good boy and please Jesus, just sometimes it was hard.

He said he was sorry, hugged his mom and skipped off with a light heart to give the medal to his sister.

Let's chat about this: What did Sammy see on the ground? Whose was it? What was Sammy tempted to do? Who stopped him? Was Sammy glad that his mom stopped him? Why was he glad?

Prayer: Dear Jesus, please help me always to be a good little child of God. When I am tempted to do wrong, please give me strength to say no. I love You, Jesus, and I know You love me too and will always help me if I ask. Dear Guardian Angel, protect me.

Sammy was taking the medal,
But he would have felt real bad.
Instead he chose to love Jesus;
He did what was right and was glad!

3. GLOOMY SUSIE

Susie wasn't happy today. Her sister was babysitting and the children were straightening the house before Mommy got home. Susie gloomily did her chores and when Mommy came home from shopping she slipped upstairs.

She had to be called a few times before she came down for supper.

Her mom asked her, "Susie, were you in the office today? You know I told you not to go in there while I was gone and now the lamp is broken in there."

Susie looked at her plate and gulped. She could hardly swallow the bread she was chewing. Then she began to cry.

"I'm sorry, Mom. Yes, it was me. I wanted to use those special pens you had in there and while I was looking for them my arm bumped the lamp. I'm sorry. I won't do it again and I will pay for it with my babysitting money."

Susie's mom and dad were proud of her for owning up to her mistake. She was sorry and she promised she would do better.

"That's okay, Dear," said her mother. "Our Lord forgives us when we do wrong and when we are sorry and we forgive you, too. Please do not disobey us again."

Susie's heart was light as she washed the dishes that night. There was joy in her heart.

"It feels so good to be forgiven," she thought. "I will go to confession and try hard to always be good. Thank you, Jesus, for always being willing to forgive me!"

Let's chat about this: Why was Susie gloomy? What did she do? Do you think it was easy for Susie to tell her mom what she had done? Was God pleased? What was she going to do with her sin? Why did she feel so good when she was doing dishes?

Remember that Jesus will always forgive us if we are truly sorry for sinning.

Prayer: Dear Jesus, thank you for forgiving us our sins. Thank you for the priests in the confessional who forgive us through You. Please help us to be good and to keep from doing wrong. Please help us to be sorry for our sins. Then we shall always be happy children of God. Amen.

Susie was forgiven,
Her heart was very light.
She smiled and thanked dear God
While doing chores that night.

4. GOD IS THE CREATOR OF EVERYTHING

One day little Benedict was riding his bike. He wasn't looking and ran into the shed. His tire was bent.

He said, "I'll wait awhile and maybe it will get fixed." Will it get fixed? Not by itself, it won't.

The next day Little Benedict was running and skinned his knee. He wondered to himself, "If I put a bandage on this, will it get better by itself?" Yes, it probably will.

The difference is that a **man** made the bike and **our Lord** made the knee. The things which God makes are much more wonderful than the things that man can make.

What kind of things did God make? He made the sun and the moon, He made the trees and the flowers, He made the fishes and the animals.

He made the very first man and woman, Adam and Eve. And He made all of us, too.

When He first made the world He said to man, "Go, take care of the world and everything in it!"

He also gave people wonderful minds so that they can *use* God's things and make things from them, like the bike Benedict was riding.

But in the very beginning it was only God who made all things. He made all the things that people cannot make. He was able to do that because He is great and wise and all-powerful.

God is the Creator because He can make something out of nothing.

We are his creatures because we were made **by** Him.

Let's chat about this: How come Benedict's bike couldn't fix itself? Why could Benedict's knee fix itself? What kind of things did God make? Who did He make them for? What did God give to people so they could make things out of what He had made? Why can God make anything?

Prayer: Dear Jesus, thank You so much for the wonderful world You have given us. Thank You for making us and showing us how much You love us by giving us all the beautiful things in this world. May we always remember that we are Your children and always try hard to be good.

The bike just lay there broken;
Ben knew it would stay that way.
Though God helped man to make it,
Dad has to fix it today.

5. LOVING HIM, BUT NOT SEEING

Sally was looking up at the picture of the Sacred Heart of Jesus while her sister, Margy, was dusting it. Her little face turned to her mom in a puzzled look and she asked, "Mommy what does Jesus really look like?"

Her mom smiled at her and said, "Well I am not real sure, Dear. I know there were saints who have seen Jesus because He appeared to them but most of the pictures we see are the way the painters *thought* Jesus looked."

"So does that mean that all the pictures are just made up?" Sally asked.

"Yes, they are just made up. You see, there were no cameras in Jesus' time so no one was able to take a picture of Him and save it for all of us to see. So these pictures that the painters created are all we have."

"Well, that's okay", said Sally. "I love Jesus anyway even though I don't know how He looked. It would be nice to know, though."

"Do you remember in the Bible, Sally, when Jesus told St. Thomas, 'You have seen and that is why you believe. Blessed are those who have not seen and yet still believe.' That story reminds me of you. You still love Jesus even though you have not seen Him. That is a very good thing, Sally, and I hope you will always learn to know Him and to love Him more each day."

"I know, Mommy. And I love Jesus because I know what He did for us. He died for all of us."

"That's right, Sally, and He is here in our churches waiting for us to come and receive Him in Holy Communion so we can love Him even more."

Let's chat about this: What was Sally puzzled about? Why don't we know what Jesus truly looks like? What do you think Jesus looks like? How do we love Jesus if we don't even know what He looks like? Where is Jesus waiting for you so He can be with You and help You love Him more?

Prayer: Dearest Jesus, thank You for all You have done for us. Thank you for dying on the cross for us and for coming to us in Holy Communion. Even though I don't know what You really look like, please help me to love You more each day. Amen.

We do not have to see Our Lord,
To know that He is there.
He guides us each and every day
With gentle, loving care.

6. ARE YOU CHEERFUL?

Daddy peeked around the corner. "Where is Gemma?" he said.

"Oh, she's helping do the dishes," said Tommy, her brother.

Daddy walked out to the kitchen to see her. Gemma was helping dry the dishes but she had a look on her face that told Daddy she was not too happy about it. Her face was like sour pickles.

"Gemma, you don't look very happy," said Daddy.

"No, I'm not," said Gemma.

"Why?"

"Well, I was right in the middle of writing my letter and I had to come and do these dumb dishes!" exclaimed Gemma.

"Oh, I see," said Daddy. "Why don't you put down your towel for a moment, Gemma, and let's take a little walk in the yard."

Gemma was a little ashamed at how she acted and wasn't sure if Daddy was going to scold her. She put down her towel and joined him.

They went outside. Daddy put his arm around Gemma. "Listen, Dear. Remember that little book about Mary that your mother has read to you? Do you remember how to become a 'Little Mary'?"

"Yes, Daddy. It said in the book that we must 'play like Mary, pray like Mary, work like Mary and study like Mary'."

"Right, Gemma. And how do you think Mary would have done all these things?"

"With gladness," said Gemma.

"Right," said Daddy. "With a smile on her face. Right?"

"Right," said Gemma sheepishly. She looked up at her daddy. "I want to please Jesus and Mary, too, so I will try harder to do my chores with a smile."

"Very good, Gemma. Our Lady is pleased that you want to try harder. Being a little Mary will make her happy and will make you happy, too. Now run along, finish those dishes so you can play with your brothers and sisters."

"Yes, Daddy!" Gemma smiled at her Dad and skipped into the house.

Let's Chat about this: What was Gemma doing? How do you know she wasn't doing it cheerfully? What did Daddy tell Gemma? Why does Gemma want to be a little Mary? After Gemma was done doing dishes what was she going to do? Why would she have more fun playing now?

Prayer: Dear Blessed Mother, Thank you for being our Mother and for the love that you show us every day. Thank you for being patient with us. Please pray for us that we may always obey and do our work cheerfully so that we can become little Marys and Marios. We know that will make you happy and will make us happy too. Amen.

Daddy talked to Gemma;
He made her understand.
Jesus wants us to obey
And give a helping hand.

7. GOD WILL WORRY ABOUT IT

Young Peter was excited! His family was going into the big city to see a play that was being performed by traveling actors. His uncle was one of the star performers!

Mom and Dad and all the kids piled in the van and down the road they went. As they got closer, and the road became busier, Peter said to his mom, "Doesn't Dad have to turn up here?"

His mother said, "Don't worry, Dear. Dad will know when to turn."

Soon the traffic got heavier. Peter looked at his mom, "Where do you think the play is? You don't think we missed the turn do you?"

Mother looked at Peter and said, "Honey, don't worry about it. Your dad knows where he is going and he will get us there safely."

Peter relaxed a bit and before he knew it, they had pulled up to the big hall where the play was going to be performed. They were even early and could find a good seat.

Peter's mom was right. He should not have worried.

A lot of big people are like that. They worry about many things. They worry about what is happening in the world. They worry whether they can pay the doctor bills or not. They worry about their families. They worry about everything.

God said that He cares for us. He said He will do the worrying for us. He is kind of like Peter's Dad. He knows the way and He will get you there safely. So why worry? God will do the worrying for you.

God does not want us to worry. He wants us to put our trust in Him. We need to pray for that trust each day.

Let's chat about this: Why was Peter worrying? What did his mother tell him? Why do even grown-ups worry sometimes? Who is willing to worry for us? Why?

Let us pray: Dear Lord, thank You for being willing to do our worrying for us. I am sorry for the times I do not trust in You. Please help me to always remember how much You love us so I will not worry. Amen.

When you get worried,
When you start to fret,
You get on your knees
And pray......don't forget!

8. MAKE A JOYFUL NOISE UNTO THE LORD

Jimmy was just a little guy and he was getting ready for the day. His mother and his sisters could hear him singing at the top of his lungs, "Immaculate Mary, Thy praises we sing. You reign now in splendor, With Jesus our King. Ave, Ave, Ave Maria......"

Mom and the girls looked at one another and smiled. Some of the notes were making them cringe. Jimmy's musical ability wasn't quite developed yet, but his joy was wonderful to hear!

Jesus and Mary were pleased with little Jimmy, too. He was singing his song to Them and it didn't matter that it was off-tune. To the Ears of our Lord it was beautiful because it was coming from Little Jimmy's heart!

Jimmy could have been singing songs he had heard on the radio. But instead he chose to sing a song about Mary. This was a wonderful thing and his mother and sisters knew it. That's why they didn't mind that he was off tune.

Did you know that singing is like praying twice? That means that if we are singing a hymn in honor of Jesus or

Mary, and we think about the words, and it comes from our hearts, it is even more powerful than a spoken prayer. That's why we should do it often. It can also help others to think of Jesus and Mary throughout the day.

One good way to learn a song is to pick one out and sing it with your family each night after the rosary. Soon you will know it so well you can sing it on your own. Then you can start learning a new one.

It is important to learn songs about Jesus, Mary, the saints and the Church. Then when we are doing our work or our play, we can sing these along with our other songs we may like to sing. We will be praying while we are doing our daily duties. It will make Jesus and Mary very happy!

Let's Chat about this: What was Jimmy singing? Why was Jesus and Mary pleased? Why is singing songs to Jesus special? How could we learn more hymns? What hymns do you know right now?

Prayer: Dear Jesus, please help me to learn more songs that I can sing for You and Your Mother. Help me to show my love for You by singing songs to You each day. Amen.

Singing pleases God greatly,
It's a beautiful way to pray.
So lift your voice in praise to Him;
Who loves you every day.

9. WHO DOES IT REALLY BELONG TO?

Susie and Tommy had permission to read Mommy's special books she had tucked in her bookshelf so they would not get ruined.

Susie went to grab one at the same time that Tommy did.

"It's mine!" said Susie.

"No, it's mine!" cried Tommy.

They both were pulling on the book when their mom came into the room. She sat down beside them.

She looked at them both and said, "Whose book is that?"

They looked at her sheepishly and replied, "It's yours, Mommy."

"Yes it is," said Mommy. "So why did you say it was yours?"

"Oh, we were just saying that," replied Tommy.

"Yes, well, it doesn't belong to you so, first of all, you need to be thankful I am letting you read it. Second, you need to share it.

"This makes me think about all the things that we have that really belong to **God.** The sun, the trees, our home, the food that we eat, our healthy bodies and minds. He gives us your daddy and the job that he has so he can earn money for us. He gives us our books, our toys and He gives us each other. God is very good to us, isn't He?"

"Yes," they replied.

"And He could take it all away if He wanted, couldn't He?

"People act as though everything belonged to them, but it doesn't. It all belongs to God and we need to thank Him for it. He lets us enjoy these things for a while. We need to share His things with others, too....just like these books you were fighting over. God wants us to share our things, even when it is hard."

"We understand, Mommy," said Susie. She grinned at Tommy and said, "Let's read this book together."

They both sat down on the couch and had fun reading the book together.

Let's chat about this: What did both of the children want? Whose books did they say they were? Why do people act as though things belonged to them? What things really belong to us? Why does God let us have them?

Prayer: Dear Jesus, please help me to be thankful for everything You have given me each day. Thank you for my home and for my family and friends. Please help me to be generous with everything I have. Please help me to use Your gifts wisely. Amen.

Susie and Tommy learned a lesson;
Mother spoke of God's great care.
They stopped their fight over the book
And sat on the couch to share!

10. MAKING OURSELVES CLEAN ON THE INSIDE

Mommy always has inspection before school begins.

"Eddie, did you wash your hands?"

"Yes I did, Mom."

Eddie showed Mother his hands. She looked at him and said, "You didn't use soap, did you? You need to go back to the sink and do it again. And this time scrub with the soap!"

When Eddie was smaller, he was nice and clean because his mom would wash him and she wouldn't miss any spots. She was bigger than he was, could see better and did the job better than he could have because he was small.

That's how it is with our sins. We need Jesus to make our souls white as snow. He has the power to do that. We do not.

When it is summertime, Mom hangs out the loads of laundry on the line. Sometimes Eddie will see the big, clean, white sheets flapping in the wind. They are fresh and white because Mother has bleached them. Eddie remembered the time their dog, Frisky, was all muddy and rubbed up against the sheets. They didn't look very fresh anymore because of the black marks!

That is the way our souls are. When we sin, it is like mud on our soul. It makes our souls spotted with black marks. We want our souls to be clean. How do we do that?

We pray to Jesus to help us to be good, we try each day to be better and we go to confession to have the priest take away our sins and make our souls as white as Mother's beautiful sheets on the line.

God is so good to have given confession to us, isn't He? He gives us confession so we can tell Jesus through His priest that we are sorry for our sins and the priest can wash our souls as clean as snow.

So, even though we need to clean our hands because they are dirty, it is more important that our *souls* are not dirty. We need a clean soul in order to be a Child of God.

Let's chat about this: Who washed Eddie clean as snow when he was a little boy? What is it that Eddie's mother cannot wash away? Who alone can wash away our sins? How do we get our sins washed away?

Prayer: Dearest Jesus, thank You so much for giving us Your Church and our priest who hears our confessions. Thank you for the gift of being able to have our sins washed away in the confessional. Please help me to remember to pray each day to be a good child of God. Amen.

Mother did inspection each day,
Ed's hands were washed and dried.
It was important for him to keep tidy,
But most important was what was inside!

11. ALWAYS GIVING THANKS

Betty was grumbling. "Why do I have to do the dishes again?" "Why is Tommy always sniffing like that?" "Why do I always have to make my bed?"

Her mother looked at her and said, "Betty, you have been grumbling a lot lately. Our Lord wants us to be thankful in everything!"

Betty was surprised. "Everything?" replied Betty. "You mean *always*?"

"Yes," said Mother, "in everything! In His Holy Bible He says, 'Rejoice always, pray constantly, GIVE THANKS IN ALL CIRCUMSTANCES, for this is the will of God in Christ Jesus for you.' So that means we need to be thanking Him all the time."

"Hmmmm....that means I need to thank Him for dirty dishes? And for Tommy's sniffing?"

"That's right, Dear. Think about it. There are so many children in this world that haven't got enough food to eat. They don't have dirty dishes because there is no money to buy dishes or food to put on them. And many children do not have to make their beds because they are too poor to have beds."

Betty was thinking. "So I need to thank God for the dirty dishes because of the food He gave us to eat? And when I have to make my bed I should thank God for my nice warm bed to sleep in? And when Tommy is sniffing I need to thank God for that, too?"

"Yes, that's right. If you thank God for all these things you please Him very much. Remember Our Lady. She was expecting Baby Jesus and she had to travel many miles on a donkey, in the cold, to get to Bethlehem. She had to have her Divine Son in a stable with smelly animals. Do you think she grumbled? Of course not! She thanked God for it all because she loved God and realized He knew what was best. You must do the same. You must thank God for all things. It will make Him happy and it will make you happy, too."

Let's chat about this: Why was Betty always grumbling? Why was Mother unhappy with her grumbling? What should we think of when we are doing dishes? What should we think of when we are making our beds? Who do you think pleases Our Lord more...the one who grumbles or the one who gives thanks? Who is happier?

Prayer: Dear Blessed Mother, please help us to remember how much Jesus loves us. Help us to believe that you are here with us and that God knows what is best for us. Please help us to be happy children by being thankful for all that God has given us today and always. Amen.

Blessed Mother, you were patient,
As you traveled far that day;
Thanking God for that cold, bare stable,
Where you laid your Babe upon the hay!

12. PAUL'S BIRTHDAY GAME

It was Paul's birthday and the children were having fun playing all sorts of games. Susie said "Let's play *Follow the Leader*! Paul can be the leader since it's his birthday!"

So Paul became the leader and all the children lined up behind him. He went outside and took them through the ditch, over the hay bales, between the thorny rose bushes and up and down the ladder to the hay loft.

The children had a lot of fun but they were tired so they headed into the house.

Paul's dad had been watching from the window. When the children came in, he said to them, "I know another game of *Follow the Leader*. Do you want to know what it is?"

The children knew they were in for a story so they said, "Yes we do!"

"Well, it's not really a game," said Paul's dad. "It's the story of following Jesus. You remember when He was on earth, He needed men to help Him and so He said, 'Come follow me.' Then Peter, James and John left their fishing nets and followed Jesus. They stayed with Jesus all through the good times and the hard times.

That is how our life needs to be. One big and serious 'game' of Follow the Leader. We need to follow Our Lord and His Church when it is easy and when it is hard.

"Did you find it easy to go over those high hay bales and through those thorny bushes?"

"No," the tired children replied.

"But you did it anyway because you knew that was what you were supposed to do if you wanted to stay in the game, right?

"Well, it is the same in our lives. If one day we come home from school and Mother asks you to do the dishes but you are tired and don't want to, you will do it anyway. It is hard but that's what it takes to 'Follow the Leader'.

"If Daddy asks you to mow the grass, and you were just planning on going to the creek with your friends, you will do it anyway even though it is hard.

"And if we follow Jesus all through our lives we will be happy in this life and we will live with Him forever in heaven. Sounds like a good deal, doesn't it?"

All the children agreed that it was a good deal.

Let's chat about this: What game did the children play at the party? Why was some parts of the game hard? How is life like this game? Is it always easy to follow Jesus?

Prayer: Dearest Lord Jesus, it is not always easy to follow You and sometimes we have failed. Please forgive us and give us strength to listen, love and obey in all that You want us to do each day. Please help us to cheerfully do even the hard things. Amen.

The children played "Follow the Leader";
Paul led them through brambles and snares.
Dad explained to them following Jesus
Leads to heaven where there's no more cares.

13. GOD SEES IT ALL

Patty had been looking at the cookies on top of the fridge all day. She knew she wasn't supposed to have one until the company came the next day. Patty wanted to be good but it was so hard!

That night, as her mom was tucking her into bed, Patty said, "Mother, I wish God didn't see us ALL the time. Then He wouldn't see me when I do something wrong."

Mother smiled at Patty, "I can understand that, Patty. God sees the good and He sees the bad. He sees what we are thinking and He sees whether we love Him and whether we love other people. It is such a wonderful thing that God sees everything because then He can help us all the time.

"We all feel like you do sometimes, Dear. Everyone does bad things and we wish God did not see them, but we cannot run away from God. He is everywhere. We cannot hide anything from Him because He sees everything."

Patty understood and smiled. She was glad that she did not take a cookie.

Do you know how we can hide our sins? We can let Jesus hide them. Do you know how He does that? When we go to confession and confess our sins, Jesus, through the priest, takes those sins and wipes them away.

Jesus is always there waiting for us and we must never be afraid of Him. Instead we need to be happy that He is everywhere and that He can see us and protect us at all times.

Let's chat about this: When does God see us? Why didn't Patty like that? Why should she be glad that God's Eyes are everywhere? What is the only way we can hide our sins? Why don't we ever have to be afraid of God seeing us?

Prayer: Dearest Lord Jesus, we know that we cannot hide anything from You and that You see us all the time. Please forgive us our sins and help us never to be afraid of You. Please help us to be glad You always see us. Thank you for your priests in confession and for giving us this sacrament to wash away our sins. Amen.

.

.

.

.

Patty was dreaming of cookies;
They looked so good on the plate.
But she listened and obeyed her mother
Who told her she needed to wait.

14. GOD CARES FOR OUR EVERY NEED

Little Freddy sat staring into space. Daddy could tell he was thinking about something.

"What's on your mind, Son?" asked Dad.

Freddy turned to his dad and asked, "How many children are in the world?"

"Hmmm...Well I don't know the answer to that exactly but there are many....millions of them. Why do you ask Freddy?"

"Well, I was just wondering, if there are so many children in the world, how does God take care of *me*? How does He even keep track of what is happening to me? With so many children to look after, I can't see where He has time for me."

"Oh, God has time for you all right, Freddy. He even knows how many hairs are on your head. Do **you** know how many hairs you have on your head? No, even you don't know that but God does. How many sparrows do you think there are in the world, Freddy?"

"Oh probably lots and lots. Probably even more than children," said Freddy.

Daddy smiled and said, "And God said He takes care of each and every one of them. Nothing happens to them without Him knowing about it. They do not fall and they do not die unless God knows about it. Don't you think He can look after you if He even looks after the little birds?"

"Yes," said Freddy. "It seems funny that He counts my hairs, though".

Dad laughed, "Well, He doesn't count them in the way you are thinking. He just knows those things because He knows everything. What is the answer to our catechism question: *Does God know all things?"*

Freddy replied, "Yes, God knows all things, even our most secret thoughts, words and deeds."

"Right and He will take care of us so we must not worry. He loves us more than He loves the birds of the air."

Let's Chat about this: What did Freddy want to know? Why? What does God know about us? What did Jesus say about the sparrows? What never happens to the sparrows unless God lets it happen? Are we worth more to God than the sparrows? Will God take very good care of us? So what should we not do?

Prayer: Dearest Lord, we thank You for always watching over us and for caring for us. Help us to know that nothing can happen to us unless You let it happen. Help us to understand that You know all about us and that You love us. Please lead us not into temptation and deliver us from evil. Amen.

God looks after every little sparrow;
He sees that they're clothed and they're fed.
In the same way He looks after me;
He even knows each hair on my head!

15. BEING AN OBEDIENT CHILD OF GOD

Do you know who the only perfect boy was that lived on this earth? It was Jesus. He was perfect in everything. When His mother asked to Him to run and get some water from the well, Jesus obeyed instantly, even if He was doing something else.

When His father, St. Joseph, asked Him to help hold a board while he cut it, Jesus listened right away and helped St. Joseph. His obedience was always cheerful and it was done right away. He never grumbled. He would even do things that He wasn't asked to do, just so He could help.

Jesus was subject to His father and mother and that means He obeyed them.

Do you think He had a glum life and never played like other happy children? Oh no! He played and He laughed. When chores were done, His little family would have good times together. It was a cheerful little home, over there in Nazareth. Jesus made His parents happy because He obeyed them always.

Jesus is God. He does not have to obey any of us. But He wanted to show us what WE are supposed to do and what will make us happy. We are always happier when we obey our parents and when we obey God. If we love God, we will want to obey our parents cheerfully.

Let's chat about this: Who was the perfect boy? How well did He obey His parents? Why didn't Jesus really have to obey them? Why did He WANT to obey them? Does Jesus want us to obey our parents? Will that make Our Lord very happy?

Prayer: Dear Jesus, please help us to always obey our parents cheerfully. Please forgive us for the times we have not obeyed them. Help us to become more like You by obeying our parents quickly and with joy. Amen.

Jesus loved and helped his parents;
He did it cheerfully every day.
His home was always happy
Where He prayed, worked and played.

16. A PERSON IS KNOWN BY HIS ACTIONS

Mother and Jenny were at the local store. Jenny noticed a little boy that she knew she had seen before at the same store.

"Look Mom, there's the little boy we saw here last time. He seems like a nice little boy."

Mother smiled and continued her shopping.

As they went by the next aisle they saw the little boy grab at something on the shelf. When his mother told him not to touch it, the young lad started to stomp his feet and make awful faces. He lunged forward and tried to grab it again but his mother caught him. She had to take him outside.

Jenny looked up at Mother with a sad face, "Oh, I guess he's not a very good boy. He doesn't listen to his mother and is not very nice to her."

"That's right," said Mother. "We could see by his actions that he was not very good, couldn't we? 'By their fruits we shall know them' is a famous saying from the Bible. In other words, we know whether someone is good or bad by everything they say or do."

Jenny nodded and made up her mind to try and be a very good girl.

We can say we love Jesus. We can go to Mass each Sunday and say our rosary each day. But if we do not show we love Him by our actions, then how can we truly say we love Jesus.

People can see whether we are good Catholics by the way we act. Are we kind to others? Do we obey? Those are the kind of questions we need to ask ourselves. We need to be a good example for others so they can see Jesus in us and want to be a part of His Catholic Church, too.

Let's chat about this: When Jenny first saw the little boy what did she think of him? What did the little boy do to make Jenny change her mind? Jesus said that we know people by their fruits. What does He mean by fruits? If someone says he is a good Catholic, and then he always does bad things, is he good or bad? How can we show we love Jesus and that we love our Faith and are good Catholics?

Prayer: Dear Jesus, thank You for forgiving us when we do wrong. We want to be a good child of God. We want to show others that we are good and happy so they will want to know You, too. Please help us to always be a good example. Amen.

Jenny went shopping with her mother;
The little boy she saw was not good.
He seemed nice at first when she met him,
But found he didn't act as he should.

17. OUR GOD IS AMAZING

A long time ago, when it was winter, there were soldiers who were marching into a town to take people away.

A little grandmother was in her house and she was saying her rosary, praying that the soldiers would not see them. She was praying that somehow God would build a wall around them to protect them from the soldiers.

Her son, who did not believe in God, heard her prayer and laughed at her. "Mother, your God cannot build a wall around us in one night!"

The little mother kept on praying.

The next morning, the son looked out the window and could hardly believe what he saw! He couldn't see out of any of the windows!

"Look, Mother! God sent a snowstorm and the wind has blown a big wall of snow against the house!"

The man now believed that God was real and that He answers the prayers of His children. The soldiers had marched right by the house because it was hidden from their sight!

When God wants to do something for us there is nothing that can stop Him. He is all-powerful.

Long ago, He promised His children that He would send them a Savior. So He chose Our Lady to be His mother and then He came down from heaven as a little Baby.

That was a great miracle! He was God, He made the world and yet He came to be with us on earth!

He did all of this because He loves us and so He could reopen the gates of heaven for us! How powerful and wonderful He is!

Let's Chat About This: What was the little grandmother praying for? Why did her son laugh at her? What did the son see in the morning? How did God answer the mother's prayer? When we pray, should we want God to answer our prayer OUR way or HIS way? Why?

Prayer: Dearest Jesus, thank You for answering every prayer I send up to You. Please help me to always know that You are answering them and that You know what is best. I know You are all-powerful and can do anything You want for us. Thank you for taking care of us. Amen.

The soldiers were coming,
Grandma was scared!
She prayed for protection;
Their lives were spared!

18. BEING HELPFUL

There is a story that Jesus told of a man on a donkey. He was peacefully riding along when some nasty robbers snuck up and pulled him off the donkey! They beat him up very badly, sifted through his belongings and stole all his money. Then they ran away leaving the poor, hurt man on the road groaning in pain!

Two different times a person walked by the man, looked down at him and then continued walking. They did not stop to help him. They ignored him and walked by very fast.

Then a kind man walked near the man. When he saw him, he stopped, opened his cask and gave the man a drink of his own water. He then helped him up on his own sturdy donkey and led the donkey to the next town.

There he paid the innkeeper from his own money to get a hotel room for the wounded man. He even paid someone to look after the hurt man until he was all better.

Think about it for a moment. If we needed help, wouldn't we want someone to help us?

Does Jesus want us to always do our best to help others? Yes, He does. It is our duty as good Catholics, when we see someone who is in need, to help them.

That is how we can be a good neighbor to others. Jesus wants us to love our neighbors as we love ourselves. In other words, He wants us to treat others as we would like to be treated.

Let's chat about this: What happened to the man on the donkey? What did the first two people do? What did the third man do? Which man do you think loved his neighbor? Have you ever helped anyone?

Prayer: Dear Jesus, please forgive me for any times I did not help others who needed my aid. Please help me to see You in everyone. Help me to know what do for others and to do it cheerfully. Thank You for all You have done for us. Amen.

No one would stop and help
This wretched and fallen man.
A man on a donkey came
And gave him a helping hand.

19. GOING TO MASS

"Son, set out your clothes for Mass tomorrow," said Mother.

"Ok, but I don't feel like going to Mass tomorrow," said Philip. "Do I have to go?"

"Yes, Son," said Mother, a little sadly. "You have to go. But, really you should WANT to go. Jesus is really there in Holy Communion and He is waiting for you to come. He loves you and wants to see you. He wants to come into your heart and give you graces to be a good boy. Do you see why you should WANT to go to church?"

"I see, Mother. I want to go to Mass and receive Jesus. It's just that I knew Jimmy was going fishing and I wanted to go with him, too," said Philip.

"Well, Jimmy is not Catholic and does not realize that Sunday is God's day. We can go fishing on Sunday, but AFTER we go to Mass. Mass is the most important thing we can do and God only tells us we HAVE to go one day out of the week. We must always put Him first and that will make us happy now and in heaven someday.

"You must pray for Jimmy, Son, because fishing will not make him truly happy - loving Jesus and going to Mass will. It will also bring him to heaven where he will be joyful all the time. Do you see why we need to pray for him?"

"I do," said Philip. "I will pray for Jimmy. And I am happy we are Catholics and go to Mass to receive Jesus."

Mother smiled, "Maybe your father will take you fishing in the afternoon."

Let's chat about this: What did Philip say to Mother when she asked him to set out his clothes? Why didn't Philip want to go to church? When do we HAVE to go to Mass? Is it good to go more often than just on Sunday? Is Jesus waiting for us to come to Him? What does Jesus do for us when we receive Him? What should we do for our friends who are not Catholic?

Prayer: Dear Jesus, we know we need You so we can be happy in this world and in the next. Please help us to always be happy to go and see You and receive You at Mass. Please help all of our friends who are not Catholic, that they will someday learn about You in Your Catholic Church. Amen.

Philip wanted to go fishing;
But first he loved God at Mass.
He's glad he put God first;
Now he'll go catch that bass!

20. PHYLLIS AND THE PUZZLE

Phyllis was putting together her new puzzle. It was a lovely puzzle. She could tell it was pretty because the finished picture of the little cottage, the garden and the tiny ducks was on the box.

She was getting a little impatient because she couldn't find the place where the next piece fit. She said to Mother, "It sure is hard to see where the next puzzle piece is and where it has to go. Right now it doesn't look like much with all these different shaped pieces laying around. But I know it will look nice when I am done."

"Yes, Phyllis," said Mother, "and our life is like that. Sometimes it is like puzzle pieces and we cannot figure out what we should do and why things are happening to us. God sees the whole puzzle after it is all put together. He sees the finished picture on the box and He knows how beautiful it is going to be.

"So, when things are happening in our life and we do not understand, we must trust in God who sees the whole puzzle when it is done.

"We will see the whole puzzle when we are in heaven. Sometimes we even get to see glimpses of the puzzle here and it makes us happy."

Phyllis smiled at her mother and said, "I understand, Mother. There is not always an answer to life's problems and we often don't understand what God is doing. We need to trust in Him. I will try to remember that."

Let's chat about this: Why was Phyllis a little frustrated with her puzzle? Why is a puzzle like our life? What does God see that we do not see? Why should we trust in God?

Prayer: Dear Lord, help me to trust in You even when things do not seem to be going right and we don't understand why things are happening the way they are. Help me to remember that You see the whole, beautiful, finished puzzle. Thank you for taking care of me. Amen.

Our life is much like a puzzle;
We don't always see the design.
We have to put our trust in God;
His plan is something great and fine.

21. ST. JOHN BOSCO AND HIS ANGEL

Mother went to tuck little Joseph in for the night. When she went in his room she found him crying.

"Whatever is the matter, Joseph?" asked Mother.

"I'm scared, Mother," said Joseph.

"Why are you scared?" asked Mother.

"Well, Jimmy told me that there are bad men that come and try to take little children. That scared me. He also told me things about the devil that scared me."

"I see," said Mother. "I don't think it is a good idea that you and Jimmy talk about such things. Let me tell you a little story. St. John Bosco needed to leave his home to help somebody. He often did this.

"There were bad men that did not like St. John Bosco and wanted to hurt him. Many times as St. John Bosco left his home, these angry men would wait in hiding to pounce on him. They didn't end up hurting him, though. You know why? A huge dog appeared beside St. John Bosco and would walk with him so that none of the bad men would go near him.

"There was even one time when the big dog didn't let St. John Bosco leave the house. As the saint tried to go out the door, the dog blocked the doorway and growled at him. He found out later that there were men who were waiting for him in order to hurt him. The dog knew it and stopped him before the men could do any harm.

"The big dog was sent by God as an angel to protect St. John Bosco!

"Do you see how good God is and how much He loves and protects us? Do you understand that He is more powerful than any bad men and any devil. Don't you see that He created them, too?

"So, you do not need to be scared of anything. God will protect you and He gives you a Guardian Angel so that you may pray to him whenever you are scared.

"Do you understand, Joseph, that our dear Lord loves You and will take care of you?"

"I do," said Joseph. "Thank you, Mother."

She blessed him with holy water, gave him a kiss and bid him good night.

Let's chat about this: Why was Joseph crying? Would you be scared, too? What story did Joseph's mother tell him? Who was the dog? Is God stronger than any devil or bad man? Do we need to be afraid?

Prayer: Dear Jesus, when I am scared I ask You to come and help me. Dear Guardian Angel, please be with me and help me to trust in Jesus more. Thank you for protecting me each day. Help me to understand that God is stronger than anything else in this world that can hurt me. Amen.

When we are scared we need to pray,
For God will protect His friends.
St. John Bosco was in trouble
And look at the help God sends!

22. LILA'S CHORES

Lila had just finished sweeping the floor and she was reading her book. She heard her mother call her from the kitchen. Lila put down her book and went to see what her mother wanted.

"Lila, you were supposed to sweep the floor and it is not done very well. There are some big pieces of dirt under the table and over by the cupboards. You need to do it again."

"Ok, Mom, I will." Lila got out the broom and made sure and got in all the corners, under the table and by the cupboards.

Her mother smiled, "Good girl, Lila. You came right away when I called and I appreciate that. Remember, you must always do your jobs well the first time. It is not important how fast you get it done, but how well you get it done."

"Okay, Mom, I will try to remember," Lila said. She cheerfully skipped off to read her book.

I wonder what it was like in Our Lady's little home when she was a young girl in Nazareth? I'm sure it must have been neat and orderly. When Mary did her jobs she must have done them very well. She probably swept the house in all the corners. When she dusted, she would make sure everything got dusted well. I bet her dishes were very clean, too.

I would think Our Lady's rule would have been "Work first, play later". And I am sure she would have done everything happily.

Let's chat about this: What was Lila doing when her mother called her back? Did Lila go right away? What had Lila not done properly? What did her mother tell her about doing her chores? Was Lila obedient and did she do it again? What do you think Our Lady's house was like? What might Our Lady's rule have been?

Prayer: Dear Blessed Mother, please help me to always do my chores right away and to do them cheerfully. Help me to do them well. Please help me to remember the rule, "Work first, play later." Amen.

The dirt lay beside the table,
So Lila came back to sweep
The rule "Work first and then play,"
She'd try to remember to keep.

23. ALL IN GOD'S HANDS

"Who is holding the world up, Daddy?" Angelo asked.

"God is holding the world up, Son. He holds the stars, the moon and the sun up, too."

"Will the earth ever fall out of the sky?" asked Angelo.

"No, it won't fall out of the sky. God loves us very much and so He will hold us up. It is like getting up every morning. God could make it so that we didn't get up. But He gives us life each day the same way that He holds the world up."

Angelo thought for a moment. "So, could God stop the world at any time?"

"Yes, God could stop the world at any time. That is why we need to be thankful for each day that we have because God gives us another day. He loves us very much and He wants us to have a happy life.

"One very special way we can show God we are thankful is by saying our morning and night prayers very well. In the morning we should offer up to Him everything we do by saying our Morning Offering.

"Then we need to thank Him for the little things He gives us.....our family, the weather, our school and everything else. He has given us life and we need to thank him for that."

Angelo thought about God holding the world up, about Him letting every one of us live another day. This made him want to say his prayers better, to kneel up straighter when he was saying them. He didn't forget his Morning Offering each morning so that He could give to God everything he did each day.

Let's chat about this: What question did Angelo ask his dad? What was his dad's answer to Angelo? Will God let the world fall? What do we thank God for each day? What is one important way we can show God we love Him and are thankful to Him?

Prayer: Dearest Lord, please help me to be grateful for each day You have given me. Help me not to complain about the weather or the things that happen in my day. Help me to see Your lovely world and to be grateful for it.

He holds the world in His hands;
He is also holding us.
We need to always remember this,
When we start to worry or fuss!

24. PETER, PETER, PUMPKIN EATER

Little Jill was running through the house singing, "Peter, Peter, Pumpkin Eater, Had a wife and couldn't keep her."

She went up to Daddy and said, "Daddy, why couldn't Peter keep his wife? And why did they live in a pumpkin?"

Daddy laughed and said, "That is just a nursery rhyme, Jill. But there are many people in this world who are poor and they have a hard time making a living for their family. No one lives in a pumpkin but there are people who live in some very pitiful shacks and huts. Their little tummies are hurting because they are hungry and the cold goes right to their bones."

Jill said, "We are really lucky aren't we, Father? We have a nice house and enough food to eat."

"Yes, Jill, we are," Dad said, "but it is not luck. It is God's love. We must pray for those who are poor, hungry and sick. And we should never complain when we are served food that we do not like or when we are a little cold or hot. It is good to suffer a bit so that we grow strong and so we can offer it up for those who do not have as much as we do."

That night Jill knelt a little straighter during the rosary and offered up her hurting knees for the poor little boys and girls throughout the world.

Let's chat about this: What song was Jill singing? What were the questions she asked her dad? Why should we not complain if we have to suffer a little bit? What did Jill do that evening when praying the rosary?

Prayer: Dear Lord Jesus, thank you for all that You have given me. Please help me never to complain when things are not exactly right. Please help the poor, the sick and the hungry. Amen.

Peter living in a pumpkin
Is just a made-up Fairy Tale.
But there's children out there hurting,
We must pray for without fail.

---

25. ST. MARTIN DE PORRES AND THE MICE

Marie was sitting and looking out the window. Suddenly she saw a baby bird fall from the nest down to the ground. The cat quickly saw it, pounced on it and gobbled it up! Marie was upset. That poor baby bird!

"Why do things like that have to happen?" Marie asked her mother.

"Sometimes we don't understand these things but we accept that it is all part of God's big plan. It makes me think of a story about little creatures who got out of control.

"This is a true story. It took place in the monastery where a very holy monk lived named St. Martin de Porres.

"The monks were having a problem, a very big problem. There were so many rats and mice scampering all over the monastery that it seemed they would take over and the monks would have to leave!

"One day the Abbot said, 'We will have to put poison out to get rid of these mice.'

"St. Martin DePorres was a great lover of God's creatures and so he said to the Abbot, 'Give me a little time and I will see what can be done.'

"The abbot agreed and so St. Martin prayed to God.

"St. Martin was inspired and said in a loud voice, 'You rats and mice! I want you to leave this monastery immediately! Go out into the barn and I will feed you and take care of you!'

"As soon as he said that, the monks were astonished and surprised as they saw all the rats and mice form lines and file out, right into the barn!

"St. Martin DePorres was a saint and so his prayers meant a lot to God and God took control of the situation. But in everyday life God uses nature to balance things out, just like when you saw the cat eat the bird.

"In the Garden of Eden, where Adam and Eve, our first parents, lived there was no worry about too many animals, too many mice or anything like that. Things were perfect and the animals got along with each other. They did not eat one another. But because of original sin, things are not perfect in the people and the animal world. And so God uses His own means to balance the world and we accept that because He knows what He is doing."

Let's chat about this: Why was Marie upset? What did St. Martin DePorres do for the monastery? What was the world like before Adam and Eve sinned? What happened in the animal and people world after Original Sin?

Prayer: Dear Lord Jesus, thank you for the Sacrament of Baptism which washes away my Original Sin. St. Martin DePorres, please help us to love and respect all of God's creatures. Amen.

St. Martin de Porres was a special saint,
He loved God's creatures all!
He ordered the mice from the abbey;
They marched to the barn, big and small.

26. ST. ZITA'S HOUSEWORK

Theresa was eating her breakfast and watching her mother put the clothes from the washer to the dryer. Then her mother went to make the beds. After she was done that, she started to clean off the table while Theresa and her little brothers were finishing up eating.

"Do you ever get tired of housework, Mother?" asked Theresa.

"Well, yes, sometimes I do," said Mother.

"What do you do then?" asked Theresa.

"I do the work anyway. And sometimes if I am very tired and I know I have a lot to do I will pray to St. Zita. Do you know who St. Zita is?"

"No, I don't," said Theresa.

Mother sat at the table and began to tell them the story.

"St. Zita was a young girl of thirteen when she went to work as a servant for a family. She was always obedient and kind. She listened even when the people were mean.

"At first the other servants were jealous of her and treated her badly. But because St. Zita was so good everyone started to love her. She stayed and worked there for many years. The poor would often come knocking on the door to see St. Zita and she would give them food.

"One day the master of the house went to see if she was in the kitchen. He was very surprised and overcome to see St. Zita's angel doing her work because the saint was out giving food to the poor!

"St. Zita died and she became a saint of the church. She is the patroness of homemakers and cooks, which means you can pray especially to her for help in those areas of life.

"So whenever you feel tired and do not want to do your jobs, you can ask St. Zita to help you."

Let's chat about this: What was Theresa watching as she was eating? What did she ask her mother? What did her mother tell her about St. Zita? What is Zita the patroness of? When should you pray to St. Zita?

Prayer: Dear St. Zita, we ask you to please help us to always do our jobs cheerfully. When we are very tired please give us the strength to do them anyway and offer it up to Jesus. Amen.

Cleaning and dishes and laundry;
Sometimes our chores make us weary.
We pray to the good Saint Zita
To help us be patient and cheery!

27. WHERE IS GOD?

Rebecca and her sister were in the car with their mom and dad. They were going to a cabin up in the mountains. They traveled the winding roads and saw many interesting things along the way. They counted the cows as they went by, they played the Alphabet Game with the signs on the road, and they stared in wonder as the mountains came closer.

That night, they were settled in their cozy little cabin and very excited about their vacation. Little Rebecca got down to say her prayers on the soft rug in front of her bed. She became worried.

"Uh-oh, Mom," said Rebecca anxiously. "What happens if God is not here and if He cannot hear me? He seems so far away here."

"Oh, God is here, all right," said Mother. "And He sees you wherever you are and listens to you. Your Guardian Angel always stays with you, too. They never leave. They watch you as you sleep. They lovingly smile at you wherever you are.

"Remember the saying, '*The kingdom of God is within you?*' That means that God is in your heart. Your heart always goes with you, doesn't it? Well, God goes with you, too. That's why we never have to be afraid wherever we are because He is with us."

Rebecca finished her prayers and snuggled into her blankets. The moon peeked through her window and the stars twinkled above. In the distance, she could hear the coyotes howling at the moon. She smiled. She wasn't scared for she knew God was there with her and would never leave her no matter where she was."

Let's chat about this: Where was Rebecca's family going? What kind of things did they see on the way? When Rebecca was ready to pray what did she become worried about? Should she have worried? Is God everywhere? Who did God give to each of us and Who stays with us always?

Prayer: Dear Lord, thank You for always being with me and especially inside my heart. Please help me to always keep my soul clean so that I will never push You out of my heart. Please help me to never be afraid and to know that my Guardian Angel is always with me and helping me. Amen.

Rebecca knelt to say her prayers,
But God seemed far away.
She remembered He was in her heart
And stayed with her night and day!

28. ARE YOU QUIET?

Chrissy was doing her dishes and the music was playing. She went to do her homework and she still had the music playing. Later, when she sat down to play a game with her brother, she put the music on again. Chrissy liked to listen to music all the time.

Her mother said to her, "God gave us beautiful music so we may enjoy it and we can have fun with it, too. I'm glad you listen to good music, Chrissy. But sometimes it is good to be quiet."

Chrissy was listening.

Mother continued, "Have you ever heard of St. Paul, the Hermit?"

"No I haven't, Mother," said Chrissy.

"Well, St. Paul was going to be punished by the bad emperor because he was a Catholic. So he fled to the desert. When he was there he got close to God because everything was so quiet.

"He loved it so much that he stayed there all by himself for many years. He lived in the mountains in a cave near a clear brook and a palm tree. He used the leaves of the tree for clothes and, for many years, he used the fruit of that tree for food.

"Then a raven started bringing him half a loaf of bread daily. That was his only food from then on.

"He stayed in that cave for the rest of his life.... almost 100 years!

"We don't have to become hermits to get close to God. But we do need to be quiet sometimes and to think about life and about God. We especially need to quiet our hearts when we pray. During the day we should have a little bit of quiet so that we can think about important things."

Let's chat about this: What was Chrissy doing while she was busy with her work? What did her mother remind her? Is there anything wrong with good music? Tell me the story of St. Paul the Hermit? Do we have to be a hermit in order to love God? Why is it good to be quiet sometimes?

Prayer: Dear Jesus, help me to be quiet in my heart sometimes during the day. Please help me not to always try to fill my life with noise. I want to get close to you so I can get to know You and love You better. Amen.

Sometimes it is good to be quiet;
To sit and read or pray...
Or just to turn off all the sounds
As we do our duties each day.

29. GROWING IN GRACE

When Ernie was two years old and just a little guy, people would ask him how big he was. He would stretch his arms up as high as he could and say, "I am *this* big!" Ernie is not so little any more. He is a big boy and one day he will stop growing.

But there is one way that we should never stop growing. Do you know what that is? We should never stop growing in grace. We always need to work on filling ourselves up with grace.

Think of a glass that is empty and we keep filling with droplets of water. That glass is our souls. We want to get our glass as full as possible and each droplet is grace that we have earned.

The way we do this is by using the Sacraments of the Catholic Church. We need to go to confession often, and to Holy Communion as often as we can.

Another way that we can grow in grace is by saying our prayers well. We must try very hard not to forget our morning and night prayers. We should say the rosary every day. Our Lady promised to give us many graces if we do that. We want to be as full of grace as we possibly can when it is time to die. We want our glasses to be filled right to the top!

Do you know the one person one earth that had as much grace as possible and couldn't grow in grace? Yes, it was Our Blessed Mother. She was **_full of grace_** and didn't need to grow in grace at *any* time. She was born without Original Sin, she never committed a sin in her life time, and her love for God was complete. She will help us to get our glass full of droplets of grace, if we ask her!

Let's chat about this: When someone asked Ernie how big he was, what did he do? Do we ever stop growing? In what way should we never stop growing? How do we fill up with grace? Who is the person who was full of grace?

Prayer: Dear Blessed Mother, you were full of grace and the perfect woman. Please help us to fill up our own glasses with droplets of grace. Please help us so that when we die our souls will be very full of grace. Amen.

Ernie is just a little guy;
One day he'll stop his growing.
If he's good, his soul will abound;
The graces will just keep flowing!

30. THE DELICIOUS STRAWBERRIES

Mrs. Jones, the elderly lady who lived down the road, had a strawberry patch that would make anyone's mouth water! The red strawberries were plump and looked very juicy!

"Did you see those strawberries, Mother?" asked Tommy. "They are the biggest strawberries I have ever seen!"

Every time Tommy walked by her place he would stop a moment and stare longingly at the juicy, red fruit.

"I wish I could have some of Mrs. Jones' strawberries," Tommy said to his mother.

"Why don't you ask her?" said his mother. "She probably would be happy to give you some because she has so many."

"I don't really want to. It feels funny. But maybe I will", said Tommy.

The next day Tommy decided to take a little walk to Mrs. Jones' home. As he looked at the strawberries, his courage began to build. He walked up the sidewalk to her door and tapped shyly. Mrs. Jones came to the door.

"Hello, Mrs. Jones," gulped Tommy. "Your strawberries sure look wonderful!"

"Do they?" said Mrs. Jones. "Would you like to have some?"

"Oh, would I!" exclaimed Tommy.

Mrs. Jones gave Tommy a small basket and said that he may fill it up and take it home with him. Tommy merrily picked the strawberries while whistling a little tune. He skipped happily all the way home, where he put the berries into a bowl, poured sweet cream over them and ate them with gusto!

Tommy could have asked Mrs. Jones sooner and she would have given him some.

Do we forget to ask God for the things we need? Many times there are things that we need or want and we don't ask God for them. He wants us to pray to Him. He is willing to give us anything that is good for us. It is true, He can read our thoughts but He still wants us to ask Him.

"Ask and you shall receive," is what God said.

Let's chat about this: What did Tommy want? What did his mother tell him to do? What did Mrs. Jones say? What do we need to remember? Does God always hear our prayers?

Prayer: Dearest Lord, You know all of our needs and You can read our thoughts. I will always remember to ask You for what I need. Please help me to remember this. Thank You for all that You have already given us. Amen.

Tommy was wishing to have the fruit
That grew in Mrs. Jones' nice patch.
She said, "Yes", when Tom politely asked;
As for the berries, they went "down the hatch"!

31. PENNY AND THE RAINDROPS

Penny was sitting at the window watching the raindrops softly fall from the sky. She looked a little sad. Mother came up to her and asked, "Is there something wrong Penny?"

Penny looked up at her mother. "I feel sorry for Susie. She is worried because her mother is sick. I wish I could help her."

"You can help her," said Mother. "Do you know how?"

"How?" said Penny.

"You see those raindrops falling from the sky? When St. Therese the Little Flower was dying she said that she would send rose petals that would fall from the sky after she died. Do you know what she meant?"

"Did it mean it would rain rose petals?" asked Penny.

"Sometimes God sent a real shower of roses when people were praying to St. Therese. It was a little miracle to show that God was pleased with her, His little saint. But I think she meant that she would help her friends who pray to her by answering their prayers. Those little helps from St. Therese would be like showers of roses falling from the sky just like the raindrops you are seeing now. So that is how you can help your friend Susie. You can pray for her. God answers every prayer. We do not know when or how He will answer it but He will certainly answer it if it is good for our souls or for the souls of our friends.

"That is the wonderful thing about our Faith. We **can** pray for others, we **can** do something for others even though it seems like there is no other way that we can help. Prayer is the most important way we can help."

That night Penny made sure to especially pray for her friend and her sick mother. She was happy that she could do something for her friend.

Let's chat about this: What was Penny doing? What was she thinking? Tell me the little story about St. Therese and the petals of roses. How can we help others? Does God answer every prayer?

Prayer: Dear St. Therese, please help us to always pray about the things that bother us. Please help us to always pray for our friends. Help us to believe that God will answer our prayers. Please take care of us and help us to be good children. Amen.

Penny was watching the rain come down,
As she thought of her friend's sick mother;
St. Therese's lesson was that we all can pray,
Which is the best way to help one another.

32. THE GRANDFATHER CLOCK

It was late morning and the stately old Grandfather Clock chimed eleven times. The beautiful soft bells made Virginia smile.

"Mother," she said. "How long have we had that old Grandfather Clock?

"Hmmm.... it will be almost one hundred years that it has been in the family," said Mother.

"Wow! One hundred years! That is a long time!"

Mother smiled, "Is it really, Virginia? Let me tell you the story of that great Dominican nun, St. Teresa of Avila. St. Teresa of Avila is a great Saint and Doctor of the Church. Being a Doctor of the Church means that she is very special in the eyes of the Catholic Church because of her writings and because of her holiness.

When St. Teresa was a little girl, five years old, she could sometimes be seen sitting by herself, off in a corner somewhere, repeating the word, "Forever". She repeated it over and over again, thoughtfully, "Forever.... forever..... forever...."

Little Teresa was thinking on what it means to live forever....to have no end. Just think about that for a moment.....having no end....going on forever.

That is the way our souls are made...to live for all time. We will live forever, there will be no end to us.

Isn't that a glorious thought, knowing that if we live our life well on this earth, we will live in heaven forever with our family, friends, the saints, the angels and Jesus and Mary! And it will be forever...no end to it!

That is why one hundred years may seem long, but it is really quite small. It is like a tiny grain of sand in the whole, big, sandy world. Think of one little droplet of water in all the oceans and rivers of the world! That is what one hundred years is like when we think of eternity!

Let's chat about this: What did the big Grandfather Clock make Virginia think of? Did one hundred years seem long to Virginia? Who was St. Teresa of Avila? What did she do when she was a little girl? One hundred years is like what compared to forever?

Prayer: Dear St. Teresa of Avila, you knew what forever meant. Please help us to remember always that forever is a very long time and to live in heaven forever is a wonderful thing. Please help us always try to be good so that we can reach heaven to be with You someday. Amen.

Virginia looked at the Grandfather Clock,
She thought it was very old.
But one hundred years is a very small time,
When we think of the life of our soul!

33. PLAYING IN THE PARK

Sharon was so excited! They were on their way to the park with Mother and they were going to play on the new slides and swing sets that had just been set up by the city.

Once they got there and parked the van all of the children ran out to get to the swing set. Susie was running fast and almost tripped over her little sister who had fallen in front of her!

Susie ran right on past and thought, "Well, good, then I'll get the swing that I wanted!"

Mother saw all this and later on spoke to Sharon. "Sharon do you think that that was kind that you just ran past your sister when she had fallen and skinned her knee?"

Sharon looked down at the floor. "No, I guess not, Mother."

"No, it wasn't, Sharon. People are more important than things. Don't forget that.

"When our Lord was on earth He spent time with all kinds of people. He took time to speak to them. He took time to cure them.

"Remember the blind man! He kept saying, 'Jesus, Son of David, have pity on me.'

"The disciples told the man to leave Jesus alone because Jesus was tired.

"Jesus was God and He had a good reason to be very busy and very tired. He took pity on the blind man anyway and spoke to him. He loved him so much that He healed him!

"We are supposed to imitate Our Lord so next time you see your little sister falling you need to stop and help her. That is what our Lord would do."

Let's chat about this: Why was Sharon excited? What did she do that made her mother sad? What is more important than things? Was our Lord very busy and tired a lot of the time? What did He make time to do?

Prayer: Oh Lord, please help me to see You in my neighbor. Please help me to put their needs in front of my own needs. Please help me to be kind and generous like You were. Amen.

Jesus had walked all day;
He needed to rest for the night.
He stopped to hear the Blind Man;
And then gave him back his sight!

34. THUNDER AND LIGHTNING

Tommy was trying to get the mower started but he was having a hard time pulling the cord. "Dad!" called Tommy. "Can you help me?"

Daddy pulled the cord a few times and the motor started to purr.

Mother was trying to move the couch so she could vacuum under it but she couldn't move it herself. She asked Daddy if he could move it for her and Daddy did. Later Mother couldn't get the jar of pickles open and Daddy opened it for her.

The next day Tommy was visiting his friend, Vince. He said to him, "My dad is strong and he can do anything."

Tommy sees his daddy doing things that others can't do and so in his mind Daddy could do anything! That made Tommy proud of his daddy and it made him feel safe and happy inside.

When you hear a storm outside do you sometimes get scared? Does the big thunder booms and the lightning flashes scare you?

When you're scared you need to remember that God is your Father in heaven and He is the one that makes the lightning, the rain and the thunder.

You see, Tommy wasn't completely right. His father can do lots of things but he cannot do *everything*. Our Father in heaven can do **everything,** anything He wants to do and He always wants to take care of us because He loves us very much.

So do you need to be afraid of the lightning and thunder that cracks the stillness? Do you need to be afraid of storms? No, you don't, because they show us how strong and wonderful God is.

You are one of His children and He will look after you.

Let's chat about this: What did Tommy say about his father? Was he right? Who can do anything? Why are some people afraid of storms? Does God want to scare us with thunder and lightning? Can God keep the lightning from hurting us? What can we do if we are afraid in a thunderstorm?

Prayer: Dearest Lord, only good things come from You, so storms must be good for us. Whenever it storms, and the lightning and thunder cracks, help us to think of how strong and wonderful You are. Help us to remember that we are Your children and that You love us. Amen.

When you are afraid of the lightning;
When thunder won't let you sleep;
Remember that God always loves you;
He's watching and will safely keep.

35. THE MONKEY AND THE BIRD

Little Jonathan watched as the zookeeper fed the monkey. The man put a pile of vegetables and fruit in the cage. The monkey went over to it and grabbed it as fast as she could. She stuffed some of the bananas in her mouth and an orange under each arm. She grabbed the grapes in one hand and a big bunch of lettuce in another. One of the pieces of lettuce fell off and she picked it up and put it on her head. She gathered up everything and went over to a corner of her cage. The monkey was being a glutton. She could not even enjoy the food because her mouth was so stuffed full.

It reminds me of a little story about St. John Bosco when he was a small boy. He had caught a tiny bird and put it in a cage.

Every day he would feed the bird something he found that he knew birds would like. One day he went to feed it some cherries he had picked off the tree. He gave the bird a cherry. The bird quickly ate it. He gave him another cherry, the bird snatched it with his beak and swallowed it up. Little John Bosco gave the bird another cherry and another and another. The bird kept eating the cherries as little John Bosco put them in the cage.

All of a sudden the bird plopped over. He lay there motionless. John poked at him. He didn't move. He was dead! John Bosco looked up at his mother horrified!

Mama Bosco looked at the bird, looked at her son and said seriously, "Gluttons die an early death."

Gluttons are people who do not know when to stop eating or to stop drinking. They eat and eat and eat and they drink until they are so stuffed and sometimes even sick.

Gluttony is one of the seven deadly sins and when we live like gluttons, our lives are unhappy.

Let's chat about this: Tell me what the monkey was doing. Was the monkey enjoying herself? Why not? Who was the saint that fed his bird cherries? What happened to the bird? What did St. John Bosco's mother say? What is a glutton?

Prayer: Dear St. John Bosco, please pray for us that we will always be careful not to eat too much and to always be grateful for the food that God has given us. May we always practice the virtue of temperance. Amen.

A glutton doesn't know how to stop
When eating and drinking his drinks.
He pays no attention to God's wise laws;
He hurts himself more than he thinks!

36. THE LION AND THE MOUSE

Mother had just finished reading the story of *The Lion and the Little Mouse* to Sam. The story goes like this: There once was a little mouse that lived in the jungle. One day as the mouse was scurrying through the trees, a lion jumped out at him and swept him up in his paws! The lion was hungry and wanted to eat the tiny mouse. The little mouse begged and begged for the lion to spare his life. The lion felt sorry for the little guy so he let the mouse go.

One day the lion ran into a trap that had been set by the mighty hunters of the forest. He put his paw down on the ground and a net quickly gathered him up and tied the lion inside of it. The lion was stuck inside the net and could not get out!

Soon the mouse came along and saw that the lion needed help. The mouse did not forget that the lion had let him go, so he chewed the little cords of the net and the lion was set free! The lion was very grateful and the two of them remained friends all through their lives.

Sam said, "That was pretty amazing! That little mouse was able to help that big lion!"

"Yes it was," said Mother. "It's not a true story but sometimes in real life God uses the very small and weak to help the strong.

"St. Joan of Arc was like that. She was a young peasant girl and God chose her to lead the armies of France against the English.

"Just think of it! A young girl marched in front of an army of soldiers, captains and generals and led them into the battle!

"She had God's power behind her and that is why she was able to free France from the English!

"Sometimes God chooses those you would not expect to show His mighty power!"

Let's chat about this: How did the little mouse help the lion? Why was Sam amazed? What did God choose St. Joan of Arc to do? Why was it surprising that she was chosen? When God chooses the weak and the small to do His work what does that show everyone?

Prayer: Dear St. Joan of Arc, you were small and yet you believed that God could work in you. Please help us to believe that God can make us brave, kind and good. Please help us to be strong in our faith like you were. Amen.

God often uses the very small
To do lofty and wonderful things!
It shows where the power is coming;
From God, the great King of Kings!

37. OBEY LIKE MARY

Mother had just finished getting dinner on the stove and was heading outside with a basket of laundry to hang on the clothesline.

She turned back to her two girls who were playing a game on the floor. "Girls, please make sure the table is set by the time I come back from hanging the clothes."

When Mother came back in from outside the table was not set and the girls were still playing on the floor. "Girls, why did you not obey me?"

The girls looked up from the game. "We forgot, Mother."

"That is not a good excuse. If you had done it as soon as I said it, you would not have forgotten. Now you will be doing all the dishes afterwards and next time you need to listen to me right away."

Obeying means doing it right away and doing it cheerfully. The girls did not obey right away.

The fourth commandment is "Honor your father and your mother". The way we honor our father and mother is to obey them as soon as they ask something. We should never roll our eyes or make complaining sounds when we are asked. We obey as happily as we can even if it is hard. We must keep trying to get better.

We can go to Mass each Sunday and receive Our Lord and that is most important. But we also need to learn to live like a good Catholic in between Sundays.

When we are children the best way to do that is by listening to our mother and father.

We need to copy our Blessed Mother. We must pray like Mary, play like Mary, and obey like Mary.

Let's chat about this: What were the girls doing when Mother asked them to set the table? When Mother came back in what happened? What did she say? Was Mother happy? What Commandment tells children to obey their parents? Are we a good Catholic just by going to church on Sundays? What must we do in between? How do we copy our Blessed Mother?

Prayer: Dear Blessed Mother, help us to always be good children. Please help us to obey our mother and father and to obey quickly and cheerfully. Please help us to play like you, pray like you, and obey like you. Amen.

Playing a game
Is lots of fun!
But when Mother calls,
You better run!

38. GOD'S WORLD IS BEAUTIFUL

Mother was taking a walk down the gravel road with the children. Colin was looking in the ditch at the soft, smooth-colored stones. He picked some up and put a few in his pocket but he showed them to the other kids first. "Aren't these beautiful?"

They continued their stroll and soon a pungent, pretty smell wafted through the air. Hannah ran to the side of the road and picked some of the flowery branches of the wild tree that was growing there. "Don't they smell pretty?" said Hannah.

Soon they noticed a cute, soft, little bunny hopping along in the ditch.

Gemma said, "What a cute bunny!"

Mother said to them, "I am glad that you notice all the beautiful things that God made, Children. Look at the beautiful blue sky, the beautiful green fields and the lovely trees that God has made for us! His world is magnificent!"

"Mom, what about mosquitos, flies and snakes? I don't think they are very beautiful. Why are some things not beautiful in this world?" asked Colin.

"That's a good question," said Mother. "It is because of Original Sin. Everything on this earth was beautiful before sin came into the world. That is what spoiled it. But Jesus came down from heaven to reopen the gates of heaven for us, to straighten things out and to help us to reach heaven where **everything** will be beautiful again."

Let's chat about this: What things did the children notice as they were walking along the road with their mother that day? Why do you think God made the world beautiful? What do you think is especially beautiful in the world? What question did the kids ask their mother that bothered them? Who came to earth to straighten things out again? And how did He do that?

Prayer: Dear Father in Heaven, thank You for making all the beautiful things in this world. Forgive us for sometimes spoiling things and please straighten us out when we are wrong. Please make our souls beautiful so we may go to heaven when we die to live with You forever. Amen.

God's world is very lovely;
We can see that every day.
If we look for the bright and beautiful,
We'll find it along the way.

39. CHARITY BEGINS IN THE HOME

Whenever Katie was with her friends, playing games and having fun, she was always very nice to them. When she saw people that she knew at the store she smiled at them and was very cheery. Everyone liked Katie.

But when Katie was at home it was a different story. She was grouchy and cross with her little sisters and brothers.

When they wanted her to play a game with them she would grumpily reply, "No!" and keep reading her book. If they irritated her with their noise and frolicking she was quick to give them a sharp word.

Sometimes it is hard to be nice, especially when we are at home with our family. They are always there with us so we do not think it is that important that we are kind to them.

It is easier to remember when we think of Our Lord and what He has done for us. It is also easier for us when we think of Mary and how good she was when she was a little girl. Not only was she kind to everyone when she was out getting water at the well for her mother, but she was always kind at home.

Jesus tells us to love our neighbor as ourselves. He even tells us to love our enemies. He always loves others and we often don't. That is why He died on the cross - to show us how much He loves us and how much we should love one another.

The best place to practice this love is at home with our family. Remember that charity begins in the home. And it shows what kind of a boy or girl you are by the way you act with your family.

So let us remember to love as Jesus loved. Let us treat others as Our Lady did when she was a little girl *especially* when we are at home.

As time went on, Katie began to learn some lessons in kindness. She started to try harder at home to play with her brothers and sisters. When they asked her questions, she put down her book and answered them. She wasn't perfect but God was pleased with her efforts. And their home was a much happier place to be.

Let's chat about this: Who was Katie nice to? Who was she grumpy with? Why should we show love especially to those in our own home? Who can we learn to be kind from? How did Jesus show us He loved us? What was Mary like when she was a little girl? Did Katie learn lessons in kindness? Was she perfect in being kind at home? Was God pleased with her efforts?

Prayer: Dear Blessed Mother, we know that you are our Mother and that you love us even though we are not always lovable. Your Son, Jesus, came to show us how much He loved us and that we should love each other. Please pray to Him for us that we may always love one another, especially our family. Amen.

Katie is nice to everyone she meets,
But at home she finds it hard to be kind.
She learns that charity begins in the home;
It is there that **real** love we should find.

40. OOPSEY-DAISY!

Jenny was at the playground with her friends. They were playing on the swings when they noticed Daisy was coming toward them to play, too.

"Here comes 'Oopsey – Daisey'!" smirked Jill. "She is so clumsy! She is always knocking something down or breaking something. We will probably have to take her home today because she'll have hurt herself again."

Daisy **was** rather a clumsy girl and that was why the girls had nicknamed her "Oopsey - Daisy".

The girls laughed and when Daisy came closer they chanted, "Oopsey-Daisy! Oopsey-Daisy!" Jenny joined in with the rest of them.

Right at that moment Jenny's older sister, Laura, happened to be walking by the playground. She stopped and watched to see what was going on. She called Jenny over to her.

She looked sadly at Jenny, "Jenny, I'm surprised at you. I didn't think you would be that mean. Mother has taught you better than that."

Jenny hung her head in shame.

"Jenny," said Laura, "have you heard the old Indian saying 'Walk a mile in another squaw's moccasins?' That means that you should put yourself in that other person's shoes and imagine you are that person. If you do that, you will treat them like you would want to be treated. Would you be very happy right now if you were Daisy?"

Jenny felt very sorry and said she would not do it again. She went straight back to the playground and kindly invited Daisy to play with them.

God's Commandment tells us to love our neighbor as ourselves. Jesus says "Do unto others as we would have them do unto us."

We need to remember that we would like others to be kind to us and to treat us well and so that is how we should treat other people too.

Let's chat about this: What were the girls doing at the playground? Why were they making fun of Daisy? Who saw Jenny? What is the old Indian saying and what does it mean? Should you treat others like you would want to be treated?

Prayer: Dear Jesus, You love all people. You told us to love others as we love ourselves. Please help us to be always kind to others even if they are different from the rest of us. Amen.

Jenny was sorry she laughed with the girls,
As Daisy came walking their way.
She instead decided to show her love,
And kindly asked Daisy to play.

41. THE PLAY CLOTHES

Hannah and Gemma ran out to the UPS driver to see what was in the package he brought them. It was a big box and it had their names on it!

Their eyes got big when they opened the box! Their aunt had sent them the prettiest dress-up clothes - one outfit for each of them!

The girls knew they had to finish up their chores first and then they could play Queen and Princess. Hannah would be the queen and Gemma would be the princess.

They were just getting ready to play when the doorbell rang. It was their friend, Cecilia, who had popped in for a visit! She saw the box and she looked longingly at the play clothes. Oh! How she would have loved to wear some, too! But there were only two sets of clothes and so one of the girls would have to share.

Hannah was older and so she knew what she had to do. She offered her clothes to Cecilia and said that she could wear them. Hannah said she would be the maid-servant. She put on her mother's apron and played being the maid. Cecilia was the princess and Gemma was the queen.

That night as mother was tucking them into bed she said to Hannah, "I am very proud of you for letting your friend use your play clothes, Hannah. God always rewards a cheerful giver. Next time when you play with your play clothes you will feel good about yourself because you were willing to give them up for someone else."

Gemma was listening and said, "Next time, Mother, I will let Cecilia use *my* play clothes. I want to be able to share, too."

Both of the girls said good night to Mother and dreamed happy dreams that night.

Let's chat about this: What did Hannah and Gemma get that they were excited about? What was it hard for Hannah to do? What did Mother say to Hannah? Why do you think they fell asleep happy?

Prayer: Dear, sweet Jesus, please help us to be generous with the things that You have given us. We know that will make You happy and it will make us happy, too. Please help us to think of others when we play. Amen.

When the girls opened the box,
They saw the pretty clothes to wear!
Along came their nice little friend;
And Hannah was willing to share!

42. DOING EVERYTHING WITH ALL OUR HEART

Benjamin was a little boy who liked to do things with all his might. When he ran he would run very fast. When he said his prayers he knelt nice and straight. When he worked for his mommy he tried to work very hard.

If Benjamin were to praise God with everything in him how would he do that? How would he show God that he loved Him? Benjamin would do it just as well as he could, with everything he's got.

That is what King David meant when he said in his psalm, "All that is within me bless His Holy Name." That meant, "I want to thank God with everything in me!"

When somebody gives Benjamin a chocolate chip cookie he says, "Thank you."

When somebody gives him a banana split he says, "Oh thank you, thank you very much! Thank you!" He is even more thankful because it is much bigger than a cookie!

Every day we need to remember how much God has given us. He has given us the food we eat, our cars, our home, our parents and our family.

But He has given us so much more than that! He has given us the greatest gift! We need to thank him with our whole heart because He gave us His only Son, Jesus. God didn't **have to** send down His Son from heaven. Living on earth was not very nice compared to living in heaven, but God did it *for us!*

It wasn't just like a chocolate chip cookie, it was like a whole banana split and even better, much, much better!

He let His Son die for us to save us from our sins and open the gates of heaven for us! So we need to thank Him with all our heart every day. We must never forget.

Let's chat about this: What was Benjamin known for? When he prays to God how would he do that? How should we thank God? Why?

Prayer: Dear Lord, thank You for everything You do for us. Thank You for giving Your Son to die on the cross and open the gates of heaven for us! That is such a big thing and so please help me to always remember to thank You every day for all the gifts You have given us! Amen.

Ben did everything with all his might;
You could say he had "true grit"!
He was very thankful for all his gifts;
He loved God more than the banana split!

43. TRUST IN HIM

Jill was sitting on the couch and watching her older sister toss their little baby sister up into the air and catch her again. The baby would break out in laughter and glee each time. Uuuuup she went....Dowwwwn she came! Up and down, up and down!

The baby was having so much fun each time she was thrown into the air and then caught in Big Sister's arms! The giggles brought smiles to everyone in the house.

Jill said to her sister, "It's amazing that the baby lets you do that and isn't scared. She knows every time that you will catch her. She knows you will take care of her."

The baby laughed as if to say, "Please do it again!" and Big Sister laughed, too. The little one knew that her big sister would catch her, she did not worry about it.

That is how we must be with God. We need to have an unfailing trust in Him and always know that He will take care of us, no matter what the situation is.

He will also catch us when we fall.

The Bible says to look at the birds of the air, they neither toil nor spin. Yet Solomon in all his glory was not arrayed like one of these.

In other words, if God takes care of even the little birds of the field, how much more He will take care of us! The birds have enough food to eat, they have wonderful feathers to keep them warm. They can fly very fast if something tries to catch them and hurt them. God takes care of them and the birds do not worry whether they will be looked after.

If God looks after those little birds so that they don't have to worry, He will most certainly look after us whom He loves so very much! We are very close to His loving Heart!

Let's chat about this: What was Jill watching her sister do? Why was Jill amazed? Did the little baby completely trust that her sister would catch her? Should we trust God? What does the Bible say about God and the birds?

Prayer: Dearest Jesus, please help me to completely trust You in my life, even when things seem to go badly. I know that You still love me and You are taking care of me. Amen.

Each time the baby was thrown way up,
She just giggled, she didn't fuss.
She knew that Sister would take care of her
Just like God will take care of us!

44. GOING TO HEAVEN

Sharon woke up in the morning and the first thing she saw was the bright, cheery sun shining through her window! Just outside the window, the apple blossoms were gently swaying in the breeze. The waft of sweet apple blossoms filled the air. Sharon woke up with a smile.

What do you think it is going to be like when we wake up in heaven? Who will we see? Who will be there to greet us?

For the first time we will see all the saints and all the angels! We will see St. Theresa the Little Flower, St. Francis of Assisi, St. Bernadette of Lourdes and many, many more!

We will see all our family that lived before us, our grandpas and grandmas, our aunts and uncles! They will greet us with smiles and hugs and we will then know how much they were praying for us through the years. We probably didn't know they were praying for us but they were.....because they are our family!

Who will be the first one to welcome us? It will be Jesus and His Mother, Mary! Our Lady will be waiting for us and will hug us as only a mother can!

Mary is very special to us who are still here on earth. She knows everything that is going on in our lives right now and she is praying for us to her Son, Jesus. He always wants us to be protected under His Mother's loving Blue Mantle. That is why, when He was on the cross, He gave His Mother to us when He said to St. John, "Woman, behold your son.... behold your Mother."

This woman Jesus was talking about was Our Lady, Jesus' Mother and your Mother, who looks upon you and loves you very much.

Let's chat about this: Was Sharon happy when she woke up? Why was she happy? What will it be like when we go to heaven? Who will we see? Who is looking after us and praying for us every day?

Prayer: Dear Blessed Mother, thank you for being our mother and for caring for us. Thank you for praying for us that we may stay on the straight and narrow path to heaven. Help us always to be good, and always to be joyful in Jesus' service. Amen.

The apple blossoms were swaying;
The sun cheerily smiled above.
It made Sharon think of heaven
Where Our Lady will greet us with love!

45. GOD IS INTERESTED

Mother was taking all the kids to the library. Once they got there little Sammy had to use the restroom. It was a very big library and Sammy's sister, Lorraine, did not know where it was.

Her mother told her to go and ask the man under the big sign that said "Customer Service".

Lorraine shyly walked up to the desk and said to the man, "I am sorry to bother you. I need help to find the restroom."

"That's quite all right," said the man. "You may ask me. That's what I am here for. It is my business to help you."

The man told her where it was and Lorraine thanked him as they went off to find it.

Sometimes people do not want to bother God with all their little troubles just like Lorraine thought she was doing to the Customer Service Man. They think that God may have too many other things to do and that He is too busy for their little things.

What do you think God would say to boys and girls who feel they are pestering Him when they tell Him their problems?

God speaks to us the same way that the man at the Customer Service spoke to Lorraine. He says, "I am your

God. It is My business to help you. Go ahead and ask for help."

God loves us and wants to help us. Nothing is too small for Him and nothing is too big for Him. Whether it is big or small He says, "Do not worry, don't be afraid. I am your God and I will help you."

Let's chat about this: Why didn't Lorraine want to ask the man for help? What did the man say? How is God like the man who helped Lorraine? How big must a trouble be before we may ask God for help? Why is God willing to help us?

Prayer: Dearest Lord, thank You for being so interested in us that You want to hear all of our small problems and our big problems. Nothing is too small for You or too big for You. Please help me to always remember that and to go to You with all of my needs. Thank you for everything. Amen.

Jesus cares about our every need;
He desires to know them all.
He wants us to always talk to Him
About the big things and the small.

46. ST. ANTHONY FINDS THE LOST

Joan and Allan were learning about the Saints. Their mother read them a story every evening about the life of a different Saint. The other day the story was about St. Anthony of Padua.

St. Anthony had a burning desire to become a missionary and a martyr for the Catholic Faith. A martyr is someone who dies for standing up for his Faith. He is a Hero of the Church! St. Anthony wanted to be a hero for His Lord!

However, St. Anthony got sick and he could not become a missionary. He was disappointed but he was determined to serve God whatever he did.

St. Anthony lived in a small hermitage where he prayed and studied. One day the preacher who was going to preach the sermon at a special church ceremony couldn't come. The Church superiors were worried because no one else was there to speak. Seeing St. Anthony, they decided to ask him if he would mind speaking.

They were nervous for St. Anthony and didn't know if the congregation would like it. They were very surprised by St. Anthony's sermon and by how well he knew his faith and the holy Bible.

His fame spread and from then on he went about preaching and helping people to understand their faith better.

St. Anthony is very special. Joan and Allan learned that he is the saint that people pray to when they lose something.

A few days later, Allan and Joan were outside, playing in the back field close to home. It was winter and the trees were blowing softly. All of a sudden, the wind started to pick up and the snow began to blow very hard. Soon they could not see where they were going. They did not know how to get home! They were very scared!

Allan remembered St. Anthony. He said to Joan, "We must pray to St. Anthony! He will help us find the way. Mother said that he helps find lost things....and we are lost!"

So that is what they did. Pretty soon they heard their dog bark. The barking showed them which way to go and it wasn't long until they reached home. That night they thanked dear St. Anthony for helping them find their home again!

Let's chat about this: What did St. Anthony want to become? Why could he not become a missionary and a martyr? How did the Friars learn of Anthony's speaking abilities? What is St. Anthony the patron of? How did he help the children? Did they remember to say thank you to St. Anthony?

Prayer: Dear St. Anthony, please always guide us in this life and help us to never lose our way to Jesus. Amen.

Allan and Joan were lost;
Too far they both had roamed.
They prayed to St. Anthony
Who helped them get back home!

47. PRACTICE MAKES PERFECT

"It's time to kneel down and say our rosary," said Mother to Gemma.

Gemma waited a moment and then turned to her mother. "Sometimes it is hard to pray, Mom. Sometimes I don't think I am very good at it. I know I need to think of what I am saying and think of the mystery we are praying but it is not easy."

"I understand," said Mother. "I think we all go through times like that. God is very pleased when you kneel and say your prayers especially when you do not feel like it. That shows that you truly love Him.

"When we do something even when it is hard that is when we gain much merit.

"Remember when you first started your piano lessons? You didn't know how you were going to get the left hand to play with the right hand? Do you remember me telling you that it will get easier and that practice makes perfect?

"It is that way with our prayers, too. The more we try to say them without distraction the better your prayers will become.

"Practice makes perfect.

"Sometimes, when you play piano, you get tired of it because you get a song that is especially hard. You don't give up, do you? No, you keep practicing until you get better.

"We may find that prayer will get hard at times, too, but we just have to stick to it.

"God knows we are not perfect human beings and that we find these things hard. He is very pleased when we keep trying."

Let's chat about this: Why was Gemma troubled about saying her prayers? Does God understand that we find it hard to pray? Is He pleased when we pray even though we are distracted and it is hard? What did Mother compare praying to?

Prayer: Dear Lord, please help me to always pray even though it is hard sometimes. Please help me to pray even when I do not feel like it. I want to show You how much I love you. Amen.

Gemma told Mother it's hard to pray;
Mother said that she understood.
She told her it was like practicing piano;
It takes time to become very good.

48. ANGELO AND THE FIRE

Angelo was playing in the storage room. The storage room was where all the canned goods were kept. Mother had just cleaned it and it made a nice little playhouse. He imagined it was his fort.

He quietly crept out of it, looked around to make sure no one was watching and grabbed a few little candles so he could light them in the room.

He knew mother told him never to play with matches or fire, but he thought it would look so neat to have the candlelight in his fort. So he began to light all the candles.

He was playing that he was hiding out from the bad guys and was quite pleased with the effect the flickering lights of the candles had on the room.

When Angelo had his back turned, one of the candles fell! It landed on some napkins and started a small fire! Angelo turned around and was shocked to see the fire! He was scared and he ran out and called his mother!

Mother came and quickly put out the fire. She said to him, "Angelo, a little boy who disobeys never gets rewarded. Sometimes even in this life there are things that will happen that punish him so that he will learn a lesson and worse things will not happen. This could have been the beginning of a bigger fire and we could have lost our house. How would you have felt then? So you see that you should have obeyed and not played with fire?"

Angelo hung his head. "Yes, Mother," he said. "I'm sorry."

"Okay, I accept your apology but you must do the dishes all this week so you will remember next time when you are tempted to disobey. You must also make sure and go to confession. Jesus is happy that you are sorry and He will forgive you."

Let's chat about this: What was Angelo doing that he was not supposed to? Why do you think his mother had told him not to play with fire? What happened to Angelo? What did Mother say to him about obedience? Was Angelo sorry? Where was he going to go as soon as possible?

Prayer: Oh, dear Lord, please help me always to be obedient to my mother and father. I am sorry for the times I have not obeyed. Please help me to listen to my Guardian Angel when he reminds me to obey right away. Amen.

Angelo was not to play with fire,
It was hard to resist this time.
He was taught a very good lesson
And was sorry for his little crime.

49. THE BUGGY RIDE

One day Susie and her family went to spend the day with Farmer Joe and his family down the road. Other families had gathered and they were going to have a potluck dinner.

After they had eaten, Farmer Joe brought out the horse with a little buggy attached. Everybody wanted to have a ride!

Little Susie wanted to have a ride very badly, too, and so she hurried into line. There were about four other children in front of her and lots of children behind her. She was happy that she was so close to the front.

Then she noticed that one of the families was talking together. She overheard them say that they had to leave very soon because they had other things that they had to do. The children were sad because they knew that they wouldn't have time for a ride. They would be at the back of the line.

Susie quickly looked away. She had this feeling that maybe she should give up her place in line and she really didn't want to. She pretended she didn't hear them.

Then she remembered what her mother had told her. Mother had said that every time we treat someone nice it is like we are treating Jesus nice, too. Jesus is very happy when we do that.

She looked up at the children and saw their sad faces. She beckoned to one of the children and said, "Here, you can have my place in line and I will go to the back."

The little boy's face brightened and he timidly took Susie's place in line.

By that time the other children had noticed what was going on and followed Susie's example by letting them all go to the very front of the line.

Susie was at the back of the line but she did not feel bad. No, she felt very happy because she knew that she had treated them the way Jesus would have wanted her to. When it was time for her to have her ride she felt happier than ever!

Let's chat about this: What did Susie want to do very badly? What number was she in line? What did she notice about another family? Why did she look quickly away? What did Susie remember that her mother told her? What did Susie do? What did the other children do because of her example? Was she sad because she was at the back of the line now?

Prayer: Dear Lord, please help me always to be willing to give to others. Please help me to realize that whenever I give something to another it is just like I am giving it to You. Help me to always be an example of love and kindness. Amen.

Susie was excited;
She was waiting for her ride.
But she wanted to be generous
So she kindly stepped aside.

50. OUR GUARDIAN ANGEL

Elisha was a wise prophet who lived long ago. The King of Syria found out that Elisha was telling secrets to the King of Israel. The reason Elisha knew the secrets was because they were God's secrets and God had told him.

The King of Syria was upset so he sent many soldiers to capture Elisha.

Now Elisha had a helper and when his helper woke up in the morning and saw the soldiers, the helper became very afraid!

"Look! There are enemy soldiers all around the city! They have come for you! What shall we do?"

Elisha was not worried. He asked God to show him and his helper all the angels that were surrounding the city protecting them.

All at once his helper saw all kinds of soldiers ready to fight for Elisha! The soldiers were God's angels that had come to help them! He was no longer afraid.

Angels are spirits and that's why we cannot normally see them. But there are many angels around all the time. And we have one special angel, our Guardian Angel.

What do our angels do for us? On some days they may keep us from falling or they may keep something or someone from hurting us.

On other days they may keep us from getting hit by a car or warn us about a bad person. Oftentimes, the angels will let us know what we should do in a certain situation. They help us to realize that our action may not be good and what may happen if we do it. It's almost like they are whispering in our ear, telling us how to be good.

Aren't you happy that the Angels take care of us? We should pray to them each day that we have the grace to listen to them. If we learn to listen to our Guardian Angel when he is trying to speak to us in our heart we will be happy and we will make him happy, too!

Let's chat about this: Why was Elisha's helper afraid? What did God let him see? Have you ever seen an angel? Who is the special angel that helps us? How does he help us?

Prayer: Dear Lord, You give us so many things and sometimes we do not even notice them or thank You for them. I thank you today especially for my Guardian Angel and for all the protection he has given me. Please keep me close to him so I may hear his voice when he is speaking to me. Amen.

Your Guardian Angel is here for you,
He protects you by day and by night.
He helps you keep away from evil
And aids you to do what is right!

51. A THANKFUL SPIRIT

Little Chrissy got up one morning and looked outside. It was raining and she was upset. She and her sister had received new bikes from their grandpa. Chrissy had planned to ride her new bicycle today.

Chrissy became very grumpy. She went downstairs to have breakfast. When she saw oatmeal for breakfast, she put on a sour face and said, "Do we have to have this again?"

When Mother told her to gather up the dishes, Chrissy mumbled under her breath, "I always have to do the work around here."

Chrissy's sister came to the breakfast table and had a happy smile on her face. Chrissy crossly said to her, "What are you so happy about? As you can see, it's raining outside and we can't play on our bikes."

"I know," said her little sister. "But I am going to do my new puzzle instead and maybe tomorrow I will be able to ride my bicycle outside."

Both little girls did not get their way, but we can see which one was happier, can't we?

Jesus wants us to be happy and thankful no matter what He sends us. Each day we need to accept the little things that disappoint us or make us sad. When we learn to accept these things we are much happier and life becomes sweet! We also make those around us happy if we are cheerful in our attitude. Most importantly, we make Jesus happy and that is what we are supposed to try and do each and every day!

After her sister spoke to her, Chrissy decided that it was a lot better to smile about it rather than be grumpy! She could see that her sister had a better attitude than hers so she decided that she would be happy, too, and write a letter on *her* brand-new stationery.

Can you see what a good example Chrissy's little sister was? Whenever we smile and try to be happy, even through hardships, we will have a happy heart, we will make Jesus happy, and we will be a good example to those around us, brightening up their days also.

Let's chat about this: Why was Chrissy upset? How did she show she was upset? Do you think that she made Jesus happy? Chrissy's sister couldn't ride her bike, either. How did she act? Which one do you think was happier? When we accept our crosses happily what happens?

Prayer: Dearest Jesus, You have given us so many good things. I am very thankful for everything You have given me and when my crosses come each day please help me to embrace them and smile through them. May I have the grace to always thank You even when it is hard. Amen.

Chrissy was disappointed;
She acted grumpy and rude.
She talked to her good sister;
Who helped to brighten her mood.

52. THE CUCUMBER SEEDS

Joey's father told him to plant the cucumber seeds in the garden while he was at work. They were older cucumber seeds, leftovers from last year, because the family could not afford to buy all new seeds for the garden.

Joey felt like he might be wasting his time by planting these cucumber seeds because they may not come up. He had read somewhere that old cucumber seeds don't sprout well.

He said to his mom, "Why does Dad have me planting these seeds? I'll go through all that work and they might not come up. It seems kind of useless."

His mother looked at Joe and smiled, "You know that is not a good way of thinking, Joe. You need to obey your father and God will bless you even if we don't get any cucumber plants out of it."

Mother continued, "Do you remember the story about St. Francis of Assisi and the brothers in the friary? St. Francis had told two of the brothers to each plant a cabbage plant, but he told them to plant them upside down. The one brother planted it just the way St. Francis said, the other one knew it was the wrong way so he planted it right side up. St. Francis ended up asking the second brother to leave the monastery because it had not been a lesson in planting cabbages but a lesson in obedience.

"So do remember, Joe, that God is very pleased with your obedience even when sometimes it doesn't make sense."

Joe understood and went with a good spirit to plant the cucumber seeds. He hoped that they would get some nice, crisp cucumbers out of it, but even if they didn't Joe knew he was doing the right thing.

Let's chat about this: Why was Joe hesitant to obey? Can you understand why he would not want to plant the cucumber seeds? What is the story of St. Francis and the cabbage plants? Do you need to obey your parents even if it doesn't make sense sometimes?

Prayer: Dear Jesus, You were obedient to Your Father even to Your death on the cross. Please help me to obey my own parents with a bright and cheerful spirit. St. Francis of Assisi, pray for us. Amen.

"In obedience everything is safe",
Is a quote by St. Francis de Sales
Joey needs to listen to his Dad
Even if the little seed fails.

53. VANITY AND ST. ROSE OF LIMA

Trisha's aunt had just sent her a beautiful dress for her birthday. Trisha wanted to try it on right away so she ran into her room and put it on.

That day, Mother noticed that Trisha was looking in the mirror a lot. She would take her brush and comb her hair and look at herself from one angle and then from the other angle.

After seeing her do this for half the day, Trisha's mother thought she should have a little talk with her.

"Trisha, that is a very pretty dress and you should be proud of it. But you need to be careful about being too vain and looking in the mirror too often. A little bit is alright but we have to guard against thinking of our self too much and how we look. Our Lady wants us to dress nice and neat and keep our appearance tidy and clean. We should not spend a whole lot of time fussing.

"There is a story about a beautiful saint, a young girl named St. Rose of Lima. She was very lovely and her mother was very proud of her. She liked to show her daughter off to people. One day she put a wreath of flowers on Rose's head to impress her friends. But Rose had no desire to be admired, for her heart had been given to Jesus. So she put a pin in the wreath and it poked her head just a little bit so that it would remind St. Rose not to be vain about her looks.

"We don't have to do things like that but we need to, first, thank God for our nice appearance and for any gifts He has given us and then not think about them too much. We must use our gifts for His service and not for our own glory."

Little Trisha understood well what her mother was saying and she stopped looking in the mirror so much. When she wanted to think about how beautiful she looked, she would send a little prayer to God and thank Him for her kind aunt who sent her the dress. By doing that she did not spend so much time thinking about herself but thinking of others instead.

Let's chat about this: Why was Trisha looking in the mirror so much? What is the story of St. Rose that her mother told her. What should we do with the gifts that God has given us?

Prayer: Dear St. Rose, please help me to be grateful to God for all the gifts He has given me. Please help me not to be vain but learn to be humble and thankful. Amen.

Trisha's dress was quite lovely,
So she looked in the mirror a lot.
Instead she needs to be thankful
For all the things that she's got.

54. CINDY AND HER SCHOOLBOOKS

Cindy was sitting in front of her schoolbooks and staring off into space. She let out a big sigh. Mother noticed that she had been doing this quite a bit lately. Cindy usually did her schoolwork with a joy and a cheerfulness that showed she loved what she was doing. But these days it seemed she had lost her love for her school studies.

Mother sat down to talk to her. "What is wrong, Cindy? I noticed that you seem tired and sad when you sit down to do your schoolwork."

"I know, Mom," said Cindy. "I don't know what has gotten into me but I used to love doing my schoolwork and now I find it hard to do. That makes me sad because it is seems so difficult now."

"I understand," said Mother. "We all go through times like this all through our life. Very often we have to make ourselves do things that we either don't enjoy doing or that we feel we do not care about.

"I'm sure you remember St. Rose of Lima. What a wonderful saint she was! Well, Rose had many temptations from the devil, and there were also many times when she had to suffer a feeling of terrible loneliness and sadness, for God seemed far away. Yet she cheerfully offered all these troubles to Him.

"In fact, in her last long, painful sickness, this heroic young **woman** used to pray: 'Lord, increase my sufferings, and with them increase Your love in my heart.'

"So you must just make yourself do the things that you need to do and force a smile and a cheerfulness even if you don't feel like it. God is very happy with us when we do that *especially* when we do not feel like it.

"One day, you may feel the joyfulness again. But until then, offer it up to Jesus and do it anyway."

Let's chat about this: Why did Cindy seem tired and sad? Do we always need to feel happy about something in order to do it cheerfully? What did St. Rose feel sometimes? And what did she do about it?

Prayer: Dear St. Rose, please help me to persevere in all my duties even when they seem boring and tiring. Please help me to do them cheerfully even if I do not feel like it. In Jesus' name, Amen.

Sometimes is it hard to do the things
We really do not want to do.
Like St. Rose we must do them anyway;
To the end we must see them through.

55. TURN THE OTHER CHEEK

"You are really dumb and I think you are funny-looking!" said Mandy.

"Yes, I guess I am," said Susan, "but I think you are nice-looking and smart."

Mandy was surprised. She only said those things because she was upset. She broke into a smile and said to Susan, "You are not dumb and I think you are nice-looking, too. Sorry about that."

Both the girls went skipping down the sidewalk to see if they could get into the game of hopscotch the other girls were playing.

Now what would have happened if Susan got mad and said something mean back to Mandy? Things would not have turned out quite so well.

Jesus says when someone strikes us on the face, we should turn the other cheek. In other words, even if someone is mean to us we need to be nice to them just like Susan was nice to Mandy.

St. Therese, the Little Flower, told this story. Whenever she went to the laundry room to do the wash one of the sisters always splashed dirty soap water on her and it really irritated her. St. Therese didn't say anything.

Instead she was sweet and smiled at the other sister. She knew that was what God wanted her to do.

You see, God does that for us. When someone says he doesn't like God or that he doesn't believe there is a God, does God keep the rain away from his crops? No, He doesn't. Does God tell the sun to stop shining on his house? No, He doesn't.

God is kind and good even to those who don't love Him. His Son, Jesus, died on the cross for those who love Him *and* for those who don't. He died for everyone so that they can enter the gates of heaven if they ask forgiveness for their sins.

You also need to be kind to everyone and even those who say hurtful things to you.

Let's chat about this: What did Mandy say to Susan? What did Susan say back? Who said the kindest words? What could Susan have done to get even? How does God treat people who don't love Him? What did Jesus do for us? What does God want us to do when someone hates us and does mean things to us?

Prayer: Dear Jesus, thank You for everything You have given me. Please help me to always be kind to those who love me and also kind to those who do not love me. That is how I can best show that I love You. Thank You for loving us even when we sin. Amen.

St. Therese loved the Sisters;
She also found it rough;
Accepting each sister's faults
And every annoying rebuff.

56. EDDIE'S GENEROUS HEART

Mother was looking out the window at Little Eddie. She remembered what he was doing the night before: asking her for old socks, drawing faces on them, adding buttons for eyes and then practicing his puppet show.

Now she was looking out the window as all the little neighbor children were gathered around him. There were smiles and merriment on all the faces of the children as Eddie entertained them!

Eddie had set up a little makeshift puppet theater made out of cardboard. He had spent all day cutting, pasting and putting together the little theater. It was a little unsteady but it seemed to be standing up well as Eddie did his performance.

He had the children laughing and fascinated as they watched his puppet play! The socks were working well as the characters of the play unfolded.

Eddie had also saved up his money to buy caramels and was planning on giving them out after the puppet show.

Mother was very proud of Eddie. He was always thinking of how to make others happy. He often spent his little bit of money on others and not on himself. He had a big heart.

Mother thought to herself that he would make a good priest. Priests have big hearts. They are servants of others and always bringing Jesus to the people.

Whatever God would choose for Eddie, Mother knew he would follow the call because Eddie has a generous heart towards others. He will also have a generous heart towards God!

Let's chat about this: What was Eddie doing the night before? Do you think Eddie had lots of money? What did he do with the little money he had? Why do you think Eddie did these things for others? What did Mother think he might be when he grew up? Why did she think he might make a good priest?

Prayer: Dear Lord, please help me to have a generous heart towards you and towards others. Please help me to think of others before myself. Please help me to know my vocation and to follow it with a generous heart. In Jesus' name. Amen.

Eddie put on a puppet show
To make the children glad.
He's always thinking of others;
He's a special little lad.

57. THANK YOU FOR OUR PRIESTS

What would you do if you had a fire? If you knew your home was going up in flames but you still had time to save something, what would you rescue?

Of course, you would rescue the things you love the most. First, you would rescue the people. Then you would worry about the *things* that you treasure.

In the old days when people were being persecuted for their faith and bad people were looking for Catholics in order to hurt them, the good people would hide their priest in a hole in the wall so that the wicked people would not find them.

These people knew that the priests were very special to them because without them they would not have the Sacraments. They would not have confession and Holy Communion. They needed their priests.

So, if the bad people came banging on the doors and broke into the home and started looking for the priest they would not be able to find him because the priest was hiding in the hole in the wall.

If the bad soldiers had found out that these people were hiding the priest, they would be killed. But the people did not care. They would lay down their lives for their priests.

We should remember how special the priests are to us. We may not have to hide them but we should always show them respect and love. We need to support them by our prayers.

We must thank God every day for our good priests!

Let's chat about this: What would we rescue if there were a fire in our home? In the old days, who did the Catholics rescue? Why did the people hide the priests? What must we do for our priests?

Prayer: Dearest Jesus, thank You for our wonderful priests! Thank you for all the Sacraments that they provide for us each day. Please help us to remember to always be respectful to them and to pray for them. Amen.

In other lands, in the days of old,
To be Catholic, you had to be bold.
If ever there was a priest in need;
Catholics showed their love, in thought and
deed.

ABOUT THE AUTHOR

Mrs. Leane VanderPutten lives in rural Kansas with her husband of 30 years.

She is the mother and grandmother of 11 children and 17 grandchildren. Her family strives to be faithful to Christ and His Church. They are devoted to Tradition within the Fold of the Catholic Church, homeschoolers, with 6 children still at home.

Their family life is lively, full of faith and joy!

44579273R00103

Made in the USA
Middletown, DE
10 June 2017